White River
Shambhala Center

The Heart of the Matter

&

The Final Words

Tsele Natsok Rangdröl

Introduction by
CHÖKYI NYIMA RINPOCHE

Translated from the Tibetan by
ERIK PEMA KUNSANG

Edited by
MICHAEL TWEED & MARCIA SCHMIDT

RANGJUNG YESHE PUBLICATIONS

Padmasambhava
ADVICE FROM THE LOTUS-BORN

Gampopa
THE PRECIOUS GARLAND OF THE SUBLIME PATH

Tsele Natsok Rangdröl
THE HEART OF THE MATTER
MIRROR OF MINDFULNESS
EMPOWERMENT
LAMP OF MAHAMUDRA

Tulku Urgyen Rinpoche
RAINBOW PAINTING
REPEATING THE WORDS OF THE BUDDHA

Khenchen Thrangu Rinpoche
KING OF SAMADHI
BUDDHA NATURE

Chökyi Nyima Rinpoche
INDISPUTABLE TRUTH
THE UNION OF MAHAMUDRA AND DZOGCHEN
SONG OF KARMAPA
BARDO GUIDEBOOK

Orgyen Tobgyal Rinpoche
LIFE AND TEACHINGS OF CHOKGYUR LINGPA

Rangjung Yeshe Translations
THE CONCISE DHARMA DICTIONARY

Padmasambhava
DAKINI TEACHINGS (Sham. Publ.)

Yeshe Tsogyal
THE LOTUS-BORN (Sham. Publ.)

Padmasambhava and Jamgön Kongtrül
LIGHT OF WISDOM (Sham. Publ.)

Contents

Introduction
7

The Heart of the Matter
9

The Final Words
93

Afterword
105

Texts Quoted
107

Notes
111

Rangjung Yeshe Publications
125 Robinson Road, Flat 6A
Hong Kong

Address letters to:
Rangjung Yeshe Publications
Ka-Nying Shedrub Ling Monastery
P.O. Box 1200, Kathmandu, Nepal

Copyright © 1996 Erik Hein Schmidt

1 3 5 7 9 8 6 4 2

First edition 1996. All rights reserved. No part of this book may be reproduced without written permission from the publisher

Printed in the United States of America on recycled acid-free paper

Publication Data:

Tsele Natsok Rangdröl (b. 1608). Introduction by Chökyi Nyima Rinpoche. Translated from the Tibetan by Erik Pema Kunsang (Erik Hein Schmidt). Edited by Michael Tweed.
Title: The Heart of the Matter— The Unchanging Convergence of Vital Points that Show Exactly how to Apply the View and Meditation of the Definitive Meaning (nges don gyi lta sgom nyams su len tshul ji ltar bar ston pa rdo rje'i mdo 'dzin zhes bya ba bzhugs so) & The Instruction given at the time of Departure ('da' ka ma'i zhal chems).
ISBN 962-7341-26-6 (pbk.)
1. Mahayana and Vajrayana – tradition of pith instructions. 2. Buddhism – Tibet. I. Title.

This book is dedicated to the swift rebirth of our precious teacher Kyabje Tulku Urgyen Rinpoche. May his next incarnation be of vast benefit to the teachings and beings.

Chökyi Nyima Rinpoche

Tsele Natsok Rangdröl

Introduction

The perfect Buddha Shakyamuni gave us, his disciples, boundless Dharma Wheels each in accordance with our various capacities and inclinations. The quintessence of all these teachings is the third turning of the Dharma Wheel, called the 'final set of teachings on the complete and total uncovering.' This is the Vajrayana approach to the definitive meaning that takes the fruition as the path, wherein the crucial points of how to apply its view and meditation training are shown. The know-how for bringing this definitive meaning into our experience is found in a text entitled *The Unchanging Convergence*, which here, in English, is called *The Heart of the Matter*.

The author, Tsele Natsok Rangdröl, was born in the snowy land of Tibet. It was through study and reflection that he first unraveled the key points of everything that there is to know. Having brought forth realization through meditation training, he became known as a great pandita and siddha, a learned and accomplished master.

Among his various instructions, *The Heart of the Matter* is both concise and comprehensible. Not only does it contain all the vital points of the Buddha's words but, in particular, it lucidly and precisely covers the definitive meaning of the view, meditation, conduct and fruition, in their entirety, so that their practice can take effect and mature in our minds.

I feel that *The Heart of the Matter* contains extremely precious and crucial advice. Since it is now available in English, I pray that everyone who wishes to sincerely practice the flawless teachings of the Buddha may take its meaning to heart and apply it correctly. This will not only eliminate all shortcomings within you but will also allow you to accurately realize your intrinsic wakefulness, the true natural state present within all of us. This is no other than the view of Mahamudra, Dzogchen and the Middle Way. May you quickly attain the unified state of Vajradhara!

Please appreciate that this book is a pith instruction, a direct path which is complete and unmistaken. Try to assimilate its meaning in your hearts to the best of your ability. Sarva mangalam — may it be auspicious!

Chökyi Nyima Rinpoche

༄༅། །ངེས་དོན་གྱི་ལྟ་སྒོམ་ཉམས་སུ་ལེན་ཚུལ་ཇི་ལྟར་བར་སྟོན་པ་
རྡོ་རྗེའི་མདོ་འཛིན་ཞེས་བྱ་བ་བཞུགས་སོ། །

The Heart of the Matter

THE UNCHANGING CONVERGENCE OF VITAL
POINTS THAT SHOWS EXACTLY
HOW TO APPLY THE VIEW AND MEDITATION
OF THE DEFINITIVE MEANING

Tsele Natsok Rangdröl

Svasti Prajnabhya

To the awakened mind, utterly pure since the beginning,

The uncontrived innate, the coemergent dharmakaya,

Which is the nature of all things, inconceivable in number,

I bow down by realizing the spontaneously present guru of natural awareness.

Sugata-garbha is present as the nature of all beings,

But due to coemergent ignorance,

They constantly obscure themselves and sink into the ocean of samsara.

So to quickly liberate them, I shall now explain the innermost, profound path.

With dread for the painful abyss of the lower realms,

Without attachment to errant paths, nor to the peace of shravakas and pratyekabuddhas,

And with the wish to attain perfect buddhahood in a single lifetime,

Wise and most fortunate ones, engage yourselves in this practice!

How wonderful is the aspiration of the one with that very name,[1]

Who asked me "Please expound upon the key points of essential training

In the view and meditation of Mahamudra, Dzogchen, and the Middle Way!"

I offer this small token of reply.

The sole purpose of the different turnings of the Dharma Wheels

By the victorious ones of the three times

Is to establish sentient beings in the state of buddhahood.

But due to the diverse mentalities and fortunes of those to be tamed,
The teachings to tame them are also different.
Since all are the activity of the victorious ones,
There are indeed no good or bad teachings.

Nevertheless, by being the support for the path, the path itself,
Or connecting you with the fruition in actuality,
The teachings renowned as the lesser, medium and greater vehicles
Are all alike in that through them you realize enlightenment.

But it is through the special quality of being a short path,

That the Greater Vehicle is exceedingly
    superior.
Yet superior to it, the path of Mantra
Is even higher and amazingly unique.

The ground, path and fruition —
Although these three are taught,
Samsara and nirvana are still indivisible as the
    expanse of the three kayas
And the ground and fruition never depart from
    being one taste.

Even though the ground is free of delusion,
In order to remove the ignorant delusion
Of being momentarily unaware of this fact,
Numerous practices of the path have been
    taught.

Their essence is twofold, comprised of both
    view and meditation;
But first of all, it is of sole importance

To recognize the very meaning of the view.

There are many types of view
Such as the uninformed views of ordinary people,
And the misunderstood views of extremist philosophies.
As they do not lead to enlightenment
I will not describe them here in detail.
If you desire to know their fine points,
Then look in the many [sutras and] tantras of the Old and New Schools
And in all the great treatises.

As for the view of shravakas and pratyekabuddhas of Hinayana,
The shravakas understand the absence of personal identity
But not of the identity of things,

So they hold on to a solidity of perceived
    objects.

Through their understanding of emptiness, the
    pratyekabuddhas
Realize that there is no object-identity in the
    perceived,
But fail to realize the absence of object-identity
    in the perceiver,
And therefore are still deluded.

The meditation practice of both shravakas and
    pratyekabuddhas
Is to train in the concentrations and in the
    serenity of cessation.
Though carrying out the five paramitas,
Their conduct is not embraced by vipashyana,
    the paramita of discriminating knowledge,
And therefore it is taught that they are in
    error.

In the bodhisattva teachings of Mahayana
There are the Mind Only and the Middle Way
  Schools.
The Mind Only has two schools: True Image
  and False Image,
And their view is to claim that samsara and
  nirvana are mind.

The followers of the Svatantrika Middle Way
Accept the unity of the two truths as the view,
While the followers of the Prasangika Middle
  Way
Teach that the view is free from claims.

All of them, however, train after establishing,
By means of discriminating knowledge,
That the meditation is self-aware, natural
  cognizance,
The indivisible unity of cognizance and
  emptiness.

Their conduct is to reach accomplishment
 through the ten paramitas
By endeavoring in the twofold welfare of self
 and others.
The fruition, [which only occurs] after three
 incalculable aeons,
Is taught to be the attainment of unexcelled
 enlightenment.

The followers of Outer Mantra such as Kriya
 and Yoga,
Hold the view of purity beyond four
 limitations.
Their meditation is to train in development
 combined with completion,
And their conduct is to maintain cleanliness
 and honor the deity.
By observing their respective samayas,
It is taught that after seven or sixteen lifetimes,
They attain the five kayas of buddhahood.

The followers of Anuttara, the Inner Secret Mantra,
Hold that the view is empty experience, and the world and beings are sacred.
Their meditation is passion and deliverance in the unity of development and completion,
And is entered through the eminent path of the four empowerments.

Through their conduct, such as utterly pure activity,
Which is the inconceivable skillful means
Of the general and specific union and liberation,
They attain, in just one lifetime,
The supreme and common fruitions that accomplish the benefit of self and others.

These individual stages of view and meditation
On all levels of the vehicles,
Are found in the countless sutras, tantras and treatises,
So what is the use of someone like me explaining them here?

In general, I am devoid of learning,
And in particular, I have neither studied nor reflected on the scriptures,
Including the Middle Way, logic, and Prajnaparamita.
So for me to persist, while unacquainted with their specific views,
Would only provoke contempt from learned people.
Out of sincere interest in the inconceivable dharmadhatu,
I will therefore rest my case.

The heart of the matter to be explained here,
Uniformly taught by most learned siddhas of the New and Old Schools,
Is that the difference between Mantra and the Philosophical Vehicle
Lies not in the view but in practicing
The vital points of skillful means.

There are some who claim a huge difference,
But, this old simpleton has found that
The essential point, the crucial meaning,
Is that although the nature of the view is the same,
Any difference merely lies in forming or not forming a conceptual attitude,
Or in having or not having personal opinion and fixation.

Although no defining characteristics exist in themselves,

The attempts to establish intellectually,

By scrutiny and conceptualizing,

The various claims that something is empty or not empty,

And with or without limitations,

Is never taught to be the view of Mahamudra and Dzogchen,

And to believe "It is free from limits!" or "It is emptiness!"

Is nothing other than straying from the view.

Rather than holding a view of mind-made assumptions,

Realize your indescribable and unformed innate nature,

Through nakedly recognizing self-knowing wakefulness,

As the basic state of what is.

In the *Noble Eight Thousand Verses* (the Buddha) says:

> "Subhuti, that being so, this transcendent knowledge fully remains as inconceivable action and thus is not the domain of common thought. Why is this? It is because it does not involve the attributes of (dualistic) mind and mental events."

So he taught. Tilopa also mentions:

> Kye ho! This self-knowing wakefulness
> Lies beyond words and the reach of thought.

Maitripa said:

> All phenomena are empty of their own identities.
> The conceptual attitude which holds them to be empty dissolves in itself.

> To be concept-free and hold nothing in
>   mind,
> Is the path of all buddhas.

Shang Rinpoche, the lord of beings, said:

> If you wish to realize the view, the nature of
>   things,
> Do not behold a view, simply cast away the
>   act of viewing.
> When free from the schemes of viewing and
>   not viewing,
> To give up doing is to reach the ultimate
>   view.

Khachö Lutreng said,

> "This is limited! This is free from
>   limitations!" and so forth —
> This view of holding such eminent claims will
>   shroud you in falsehood.
> In the ordinary view of simply *what is*,
> You see no 'thing' and yet it is seen.

He continues:

> The two truths of the learned scholar

May be full of logic and citations but miss
   the vital point.
To split it in two spoils nonduality,
And forever spins the conceptual machine
   that accepts and rejects.

There is an untold number of such quotations.

༄༅༅

In the great chariots of the traditions of
   Maitreya and Manjushri,
Who unraveled the intents of the middle and
   final Wheels taught by the Buddha,
And in the philosophical systems known as the
   Middle Way and Mind Only,
Of their successors Asanga, Nagarjuna, and so
   forth,
How can there possibly ever be any faults!

Although there is not the slightest disharmony

Between them and the meaning of Mahamudra and Dzogchen,
There have been many people in later times whose pretense of scholarship
Polluted the Middle Way and Mind Only by tainting it with their personal inventions.

Their manifold arguments to prove or disprove a maxim,
Regardless of how lofty the understanding of such an established view may be,
Will not result in realization of self-existing wakefulness, simply as it is,
Let alone enlightenment.
But without reducing disturbing emotions in the least,
They swell with intellectual pretension and the pride of vast learning,
Heading for disaster by using the Dharma to create rebirth in the lower realms.

Saraha, the great brahmin, said:

> Those who don't drink their fill
> From the cool and soothing nectar of their
>   master's oral instructions,
> Will only be tortured by thirst
> On the desert plains of countless treatises.

For this reason, it is essential

Not to pursue nor cling to views proven only by words,

But to personally begin training in the view and meditation

Of the lineage of profound meaning.

You may wonder if the prelude to meditation,
 the various ways of seeking the mind,
Isn't a conceptualized form of analysis.
Well it isn't, since its source, dwelling and
 disappearance
Are all realized through the knowledge
 resulting from meditation,
By your master's blessings and within your
 mind's composure,
And is not the pursuit of the shifting intellect.

The dry theory of conceptualizing
Through endless speculations and lists of
 contradictions,
Is in no way equal to seeing the nature of your
 mind.

Well, you may now wonder, "What is the actual view of seeing your own nature through the traditions of these profound paths?"

༃༄

The Middle Way, the unity of the two truths
    beyond limitations,
Mahamudra, the basic wakefulness of the
    uncontrived natural state,
And the Great Perfection, the original
    Samantabhadra of primordial purity —
Are all in agreement on a single identical
    meaning.

This mind that is present in all beings
Is in essence an original emptiness, not made
    out of anything whatsoever.
By nature it is unimpeded experience, aware
    and cognizant.

Their unity, unfathomable by the intellect,
Defies such attributes as being present or absent, existent or nonexistent, permanent or nothingness.

Spontaneously present since the beginning, yet not created by anyone,
This self-existing and self-manifest natural awareness, your basic state,
Has a variety of different names:
In the Prajnaparamita vehicle it is called innate truth.
The vehicle of Mantra calls it natural luminosity.
While a sentient being it is named sugata-garbha.
During the path it is given names which describe the view, meditation, and so forth.
And at the point of fruition it is named dharmakaya of buddhahood.

All these different names and classifications
Are nothing other than this present ordinary mind.

༄༅

Before being spoiled by delusion it is called primordial purity.
When deluded and covered by defilement it is named all-ground.

The moment you recognize the falsity of delusion is called the view.
To sustain that recognition undistractedly is known as meditation.
To be undeluded throughout daily activities is named conduct.
When habitual tendencies and delusion are purified is called fruition.

Thus this single mind itself
Receives endless names and classifications
Due to the different situations of ground, path and fruition.

The eloquent ocean-like words of the buddhas
Are all given solely for the purpose of realizing this nature.
Still people are bewildered and confuse themselves
With all these names and words.

Being indivisibly cognizant, aware and empty,
This mind itself holds no duality of seer and seen.
To see this is called realizing the natural state of the view.

Setting aside the blessings of the true transmission, the element of devotion,

Neither perfecting the accumulations nor
 purifying the obscurations,
Someone endowed with a lucid memory, vast
 learning,
And brilliant scrutiny is still unable to realize
 this nature.
It requires a worthy person with the right
 karmic potential.

※

The siddha Luhipa said it like this:

> You should regard the phenomena of samsara
> and nirvana
> Neither as concrete nor abstract, nor as both
> or neither.
> That which is hard to point out to a childish
> person results from serving a master,
> Once you discover it through him, you will
> see this unseen nature.

In the vajra songs of Tilopa you find this:

This intrinsic and innate wakefulness
Remains at the very heart of all beings.
And yet, it is never perfected without being
    pointed out by a master.

The incomparable Gampopa continues:

Not the domain of the ordinary person,
Nor known by someone of great learning,
It is understood by the devoted,
Depends on the path of blessings,
And is supported by the master's words.

Gyalwa Drigungpa said:

Secret Mantra is the path of blessings.
Unless you receive a master's blessings,
Whatever you realize is constructed by
    thought.
And thought is taught to be superficial and
    obscuring.
Therefore serve a master
And supplicate him tirelessly.

Thus the way to unmistakenly realize the view, the nature of the basic state, depends upon devotion and blessings.

༄༅

Having thus seen the nature of the view,
How then should one practice?

In the case of the lower vehicles
You are taught to establish the view as emptiness
By analyzing with discriminating knowledge.
The practice is to then train in combining emptiness and compassion
And to endeavor in gathering accumulations and purifying obscurations.

Commonly, both the outer and inner Secret Mantra
Teach you to train, as a unity,

In the development stage of deity yoga
And the completion stage with and without attributes
Within the state that is sealed with the view.

It is indeed wonderful that,
Being ingenious at using skillful means,
The buddhas have taught
All these different classifications
To influence disciples with complex inclinations.

However, in this context, the practice of Mahamudra and Dzogchen,
The very pinnacle of vehicles,
Is not at all like these other teachings
In which their meditations and the view remain disconnected.

Here the view and meditation are not kept separate

But are simply an indivisible unity:
The view of seeing your basic state,
Not by fabricating it, but by allowing it to resume its natural flow.

According to people's different capacities,
For the highest, the unity of shamatha and vipashyana
Is pointed out from the very first.
There is no need to compose the meditation state and pursue the post-meditation.
Instead, realization and liberation are simultaneous
Within the all-pervasive expanse of your innate nature.

For those of you with medium and lesser capacities, in common,
Bring forth signs by means of the preliminary practices,
And then thoroughly resolve the view.

When you are easily able to see the nature of mind,

Maintain the quality of stillness.

Deeply relaxing body, speech and mind,

Don't pursue any thoughts about past or future,

But allow your present wakefulness to look directly into itself.

Neither inhibit nor indulge

The six sense impressions of sights, sounds, smells, and so forth.

Towards every experience, whatever takes place,

Be awake, lucid, and fresh

While maintaining a balance between being collected and relaxed.

When too concentrated, you manufacture a state.

When too lax, you diffuse into the undercurrent of thought.

Instead, to simply remain undistracted
Is itself the supreme shamatha
Which is taught to be the foundation for meditation training.

These days, there seem to be some practitioners of shamatha
Who regard the state of nonthought in which the six senses are shut down
As the most eminent.
This is called the 'serenity of cessation',
And it is taught to be a flaw and side-track of meditation training,
Which only results in a rebirth in either a formless realm
Or as a naga or an animal.
Either way, it never leads to liberation.

༄༅༄

This indeed is what Lord Sakyapa meant when he said:

> It is taught that fools who train in
>   'Mahamudra'
> Mainly cause [rebirth as] an animal.
> If not, they take rebirth in the formless
>   realms,
> Or else they fall into the cessation of a
>   shravaka.

In any case, all sutras and tantras emphasize that enlightenment is never attained through stubbornly training in nonthought by suppressing thought activity. The *Lalita Vistara* phrases it like this:

> When embarking upon true enlightenment,
>   Shakyamuni, the Tathagata,
> Formed the resolve to attain buddhahood
>   through emptiness.
> When at the banks of Nairanjana, he
>   remained in motionless samadhi,
> The conqueror Immutable Sky appeared
>   filling the sky like a full sesame pod.
> Snapping his fingers at the son of the
>   conquerors, he spoke in verse:

> "This meditation state is not the perfect one.
> Through it you will not attain the ultimate.
> Instead bring to mind the most eminent
>   luminosity, like the expanse of the sky!"

The story continued:

> When he heard these words he abandoned the motionless samadhi.

Thus it is taught in great detail.

There is also the story about how Nyang Ben Tingdzin Zangpo once received instruction in meditation from a Chinese Hashang teacher. Practicing assiduously, he had many visions including conditioned types of superknowledge. Impressed with his own excellent meditation, he met the great pandita Vimalamitra and said, "Due to my samadhi I can remain immersed for many days without any thought of food or drink." Vimalamitra responded with displeasure, "Through that you will take rebirth as a *naga*. It's useless!" Nyang Ben then began to follow the great pandita, requested the Great Perfection from him and, by practicing it, attained the body of light.

When Lord Gampopa related to Milarepa how he had had excellent samadhi experiences through meditating using the Kadam instructions, Milarepa laughed and said, "You don't get butter from squeezing sand. Instead of that, practice this instruction of mine."

There are many such stories, so apart from the supreme type of shamatha, it is obviously essential that we don't become involved in the inferior types of shamatha or the shamatha of cessation.

※

Therefore, do not inhibit any experience
Such as the six sense impressions,
And don't stray into fixating or indulging.
If you endeavor in this supreme shamatha
Of resting loosely in the composure of naturalness,
You will have the experiences of movement, attainment,

Familiarization, stability and perfection.

It is exceedingly important that
No matter how many superficial, conditioned qualities you have -
Such as experiences of bliss, clarity and nonthought,
Superknowledges, visions, miraculous powers, and so forth -
You should not get involved in feeling conceited,
Fascinated, attached or proud.
Yet, even so, I have seen many meditators who became seduced
By such experiences, visions, and signs on the path.

༃༃

The sugata Phagmo Drubpa said:

> Without experiencing luminosity free from fixation,
> One clings to the meditation-moods of bliss and clarity.
> It is useless to meditate with a conceptual frame of mind
> Won't it only create a rebirth as a formless god?

He also said:

> The person of great power and ability
> Ends up performing endless rituals for pay.
> The meditator with [attachment to] clear dreams
> Invokes enslavement by evil spirits[2]

Milarepa said:

> When even evil spirits and non-Buddhists
> Possess such common and fleeting qualities,
> Without the realization of nonduality
> How can these possibly suffice to make you a siddha?

Consequently, there is no fault greater than this evil spirit of ego-clinging.

ॐ☸ॐ

Therefore, when you become adept in the flawless shamatha
You stabilize the foundation for meditation training.

The original wakefulness of vipashyana belonging to the main part
Depends exclusively on having or not having
Received the blessings and pointing-out instruction.
Apart from that, even the thoughts of worldly folk
Are indeed vipashyana manifest as conceptual thinking.

Even that which sustains the meditation state
of shamatha
Is nothing other than vipashyana.
That which sees, notices, or feels
Whether there is stillness or movement,
distraction or no distraction,
Is also the cognizant wakefulness of
vipashyana.

There is no other vipashyana superior to this
Which needs to be separately accomplished.
Therefore, from the very outset,
The supreme shamatha and vipashyana
Co-exist and are spontaneously present.

※

For this reason, the vital point that the shamatha of cessation by suppressing sensations is ineffective is due to the fault that it blocks off vipashyana. The qualities of realizing the ultimate fruition, all the unique attributes of buddhahood, the 37 qualities that are aspects of enlightenment, and so forth, as well as the virtues of the twofold supreme knowledge, are all exclusively the outcome of vipashyana. Consequently, no matter how stable you become in the shamatha that suppresses vipashyana, you will not be liberated. That is both the reason and the crucial point.

༄༅༔

Whether your mind is still or whether it moves,
Whatever state it happens to be in,
In essence, it is an unidentifiable freshness,
That has neither color, shape, nor attributes.
And yet, its unobstructed cognizance is wide awake.

Whatever thought unfolds, whether good or evil,

THE HEART OF THE MATTER

It is an utter openness, made out of nothing concrete.

In any of the six sense impressions, whatever is experienced,

It is totally insubstantial, with no clinging to solidity.

Without sinking into dull mindlessness,

It is utter brilliance, aware and awake.

To recognize the natural face of this ordinary mind,

Uncorrupted by the meditation-moods of bliss, clarity and emptiness,

Is known as vipashyana, clear seeing.

Unanimously this is the very heart

Of Mahamudra, the Middle Way, Pacifying, and Cutting.

So simply recognize that alone!

This is exactly what in all the philosophical vehicles is called the 'vipashyana that discerns and fully realizes phenomena, just as they are.' Nevertheless, it is rare that someone actually brings it into personal experience rather than feeling it is sufficient to just leave it as only a name or theory.

In the context of emphasizing the 'path of means' within the vehicle of Secret Mantra, it is known as 'intrinsic wakefulness of empty bliss' and by other such names. In the context of the 'path of liberation' such as Mahamudra, Dzogchen, Pacifying, Cutting, and so forth, this type of vipashyana is called the 'vipashyana which knows the thatness of mind as it is'.

After having finally realized it, at the time of nonmeditation of the Mahamudra system or 'culmination of awareness' according to Dzogchen, it is called the 'vipashyana that realizes the innate nature exactly as it is'.

Understand that these three types of vipashyana are all included within simply recognizing the natural face of your present ordinary mind.

I have now described both the flaws and qualities of shamatha, as well as the nature of vipashyana. I have also described how the supreme shamatha and vipashyana are indivisible and how to sustain this unity. Without a doubt this is the description of the main part of meditation.

Nevertheless, in accordance with the general approach of the teachings, I shall now express once more, as a brief hint, how to proceed on a daily basis with the actual practice.

࿇

When someone has reached stability in shamatha

Or, if not, at least gained some degree of certainty,

How do they then continue the daily practice?

The different approaches of the various guidance manuals

Teach us to seek the 'meditation through the view' or the 'view through meditation'.

As the intent and purpose is the same,

In any of these various systems outlining the sequence or order

For 'mind-search' and shamatha training that you happen to follow,

They are always identical in meditation and post-meditation.

The guidance in the view of the Middle Way

Teaches that the meditation state is to train exclusively in emptiness,

While in the post-meditation you cultivate

Loving kindness and compassion, like a magical illusion.

In that system, the meditation state is called 'space-like dhyana'

And the post-meditation 'magical samadhi'.

About this, Lord Gampopa said:

> The followers of the Paramita vehicle train in meditation after establishing, by means of scriptures and reasoning, that dependent origination and so forth are experienced while being devoid of a self-nature. Thus they create emptiness out of devoted interest. This is the meditation system of the Middle Way which means there is a dualistic attitude involved in holding the notions of meditator and meditation object. Through this you don't realize the view. Because of counteracting the fixation on concreteness, it can purify boundless obscurations, but it cannot bring enlightenment.

He continued:

> Others briefly place themselves in the meditation on complete nonthought and train in the post-meditation as being dream and magical illusion. In the system of Guru Milarepa, you train in the five poisons and in

R.

Tsele Nabok Ransirel
The Heart of the Matter

every thought being nondual wakefulness.
Once adept, you train in nothing but the
meditation state beyond sessions and breaks.

Thus he taught in great detail.

☙❧

In all Mahamudra systems, the beginning yogis
Make the meditation state the main part of the sessions
While the post-meditation is to sustain it with mindfulness during the activities of the breaks.
Once they have realized some degree of familiarization,
It is taught that everything then becomes purely the meditation state.

Dzogchen systems, for the most part,

Being intended for the instantaneous type of person,
Teach while condensing everything into the dividing point between knowing and not knowing,
Rather than dividing between meditation and post-meditation.

Whichever is the case, the crucial point in the practice
Is not to get involved in deliberately projecting or concentrating
Upon the state of your present naked mind,
But rather, simply to recognize your nature in whatever you experience, no matter what it is.
That which sustains this is given the name 'mindfulness'.
Although in shamatha an emphasis on stillness is taught,

At this point you bring everything into the
 training, be it stillness or thinking.

Whether your thoughts manifest as 'evil',
Such as the five poisonous emotions, pain, and
 sickness,
Or in the various forms of goodness,
Such as devotion and compassion,
 renunciation and pure perception,
Whatever you experience, realize that all of it
Is simply the unobstructed play of your own
 mind.
Without rejecting with anger or accepting with
 attachment,
Rest loosely in the innate state of same taste.

Let go into your natural state, with no need to
 cling to or fixate on
Even the impetus or the attitude "I meditate!"
Without disturbing yourself with any ambition,

Such as hoping for a good meditation or
    fearing it won't succeed,
To let be in unfabricated naturalness free from
    concepts,
Is the meditation state of all the systems of
    definitive meaning.

※

It is deluded fixation to cling to solid reality
While you walk, sit, eat, lie down or talk.
But when you never separate yourself from the
    training during any daily activity,
Simply recognizing your nature, while
    remaining undistracted,
Is still the meditation state itself, even though
    it may be called 'post-meditation'.

Unless you know how to sustain the natural
    mode of your innate nature,

You may keep the posture and gaze, but it still isn't meditation.

In short, as long as you embrace whatever you experience with a sense of wakefulness,

All you do is meditation training.

But if not, though your stillness may be steady, it is only a blocked state of indifference.

Therefore, simply sustain the recognition of ordinary mind.

☙❦❧

In the *Sutra on Pure Intention* you find this passage:

> Manjushri asked, "What is a meditating monk's experience of samadhi?"
>
> The [Buddha] replied, "It is like the smoke from a chimney ceasing when the flames in the fireplace are extinguished. Once he understands and sees that mind is empty, he will have the experience that visual

forms are empty appearance, sounds are empty resounding, smells are empty sensation, flavors are empty tasting, and textures are empty feeling. Thus, the sky clears when not obscured; water clears when not stirred up; and mind eases when not contrived."

He continued:

> The monk who knows the nature of mind
> Continues the meditation training, no
>   matter what he does;
> He remains in the innate nature.

If you can abide by sustaining what he taught, you will have no great difficulty in maintaining a continuous meditation state.

Furthermore, you don't need to suppress thought movement, the six sense impressions and so forth, as the Dzogchen scriptures mention:

> When the mind's fixating thought
> Does not engage in the lucid cognitions of
>   the five senses,
> This itself is the buddha mind.

You also find this quotation:

> The pleasures and painful states you have in dreams
> Are all of an equal nature the moment you wake up.
> Likewise, the states of thought and nonthought
> Are of equal nature in the moment of awareness.

In the *Dzogchen Hearing Lineage of Aro* you find this:

> Like the analogy of a cloud in the sky,
> While your mind creates projections
> They appear but don't harm its basic ground.
> Similarly, within the awakened state of mind,
> Thoughts don't obscure and need not be corrected.

The Golden Garland of Rulu mentions:

> The yogi who realizes this
> Will rest his mind in unfabricated freshness;
> So don't block off your senses but rest them in their natural state.

> Sight, sound, smell, taste and texture —
> In whatever you see and whatever you experience,
> Compose yourself freely in the state of simply that.
> Without inhibiting and without holding on,
> Remain in equanimity, the state of awareness.

There are innumerable similar quotations. Since all the 6,400,000 tantras of the Great Perfection unanimously teach this very same crucial point, why should I keep citing more quotes? Similarly, all the scriptures on Mahamudra have nothing other than this same basic intent. This is why the glorious Shavaripa said:

> Cutting to its root, mind is like the sky.
> It is not some 'thing' to be cultivated, so don't mentally form it.
> Just like space cannot observe space,
> Likewise emptiness cannot imagine emptiness.

He also sang:

In this way, at any moment throughout the
    three times,
To simply sustain the boundless innate state
    of nondoing mind,
Is given the name 'meditation'.
Don't control the breath, don't tie down
    thought,
But rest your mind uncontrived, like a small
    child.

When starting to think, look into that itself.
Don't conceive of the wave being different
    from the water.
Within the Mahamudra of nondoing mind,
There is not even a speck of dust to be
    meditated forth, so don't create
    something by meditating.
The supreme meditation is to never depart
    from the nature of nonmeditation.

The glorious Naropa said:

> When looking, look into your own mind.
> Since this mind is not made out of anything,
> Indescribable, and beyond any object,
> It is unconstructed, like the sky.

Lord Marpa sang:

> In general, no matter how the perceived is seen,
> When not realized, it is a deluded perception
> And tied down by clinging to outer objects.
> For the realized, it is seen as a magical illusion,
> So perceived objects dawn as helpers.
> In the ultimate sense there is never any perception;
> It is utterly freed into nonarising dharmakaya.
>
> Within, this consciousness of moving thoughts,
> When not realized, is ignorance,
> The basis for karma and disturbing emotions.
> When realized, it is a self-knowing wakefulness,
> Which perfects all virtuous qualities.
> In the ultimate sense, since all phenomena are brought to exhaustion,

It is taught that original wakefulness doesn't really exist.

The conqueror Götsangpa said:

Look directly into your own mind.
When looking it is unseen and inconcrete.
Rest loosely in this absence.
Remain free and easy, without fixation.

When once again a thought begins to move,
Recognize its nature directly,
And rest loosely in simply that.
Beyond a doubt, it dissolves into itself.

The siddha Orgyenpa sang:

During the experience of ordinary mind,
While practicing, undistracted like the
    continuos flow of a river,
Let loose your mind,
Unbridled and without any fabrication be
    utterly free.

To summarize, all the scriptures and instructions of Mahamudra and Dzogchen, as well as all the oral advice of the lineage masters, exclusively teach how to continue the training with no difference between stillness and thought occurrence. Likewise, they also describe nothing other than how to use sense perceptions, thoughts and so on, as helpers without rejecting them.

Although this is so, I see that nowadays there are still a predominant number of meditators, of both the New and Old schools, who understand the word 'nondistraction' to mean that meditation is to sustain a state of stillness and that everything else is not meditation training. After this, they set their minds on nothing but shamatha.

Therefore, I feel that not only are we at a time when the Vinaya teachings and the practice of the general tradition of Secret Mantra, for the most part, are being distorted and are in decline, but even the teachings of the Practice Lineage are close to fading away.

ॐ

This basic state of originally pure natural
  awareness
Is unseen by oneself, like the treasure in a poor
  man's house.
Once you realize it through the guru's
  kindness,
You personally know the indivisible three kayas
  to be your own nature.

At that moment, the view, meditation, conduct
  and fruition, the paths, bhumis and so on,
All these many classifications with delectable
  names,
By resolving their root, the heart of the matter,
You cut through the hope of success and the
  fear of failure.

If you begin to desire the gifts of experiences
  and insights, signs and indications of
  progress,

You are already possessed by attachment and
    ego-clinging,
And there will never be a chance for
    meditation training.

While the qualities of samsara and nirvana are
    spontaneously present in the ground,
Failing to acknowledge this, to hanker after
    the signs of the path as well as a result,
Is far inferior to even the Hinayana.
All side-tracks, obscurations, and obstacles
    arise from this.

A person who understands that samsara and
    nirvana are both mind,
Is free from the basis for any occurrence
Of side-tracks, deviations, and mistakes,
And will therefore possess the qualities of
    fruition, effortlessly and spontaneously.

Tilopa described it in these words:

> When you realize the equal nature
> Of these three: view, meditation and
>   conduct,
> There is no duality of good and evil.
> But if you hold some other thought,
> You have no confidence and are deluded.

Gampopa also said:

> For the view, free from change,
> Have a realization that cuts through ground
>   and root.
> For the meditation, free from sessions and
>   breaks,
> Remain continuously throughout the three
>   times.
>
> For the conduct, free from hypocrisy,
> Possess an altruism that is not self-seeking.
> For the fruition, free from hope and fear,
> Bring your training to perfection.

The shortcoming of expecting to quickly have signs of progress or experience and realization and other qualities, without having cut through the ego-oriented frame of mind, is described by the accomplished master Lingje Repa:

> If you wish to see the buddha mind,
> Hankering after signs of progress only postpones it.
> Once your wishing for signs of progress is exhausted,
> You have arrived at the buddha mind.

He also said:

> As long as you retain conceptual clinging,
> You will never cross the river of samsara.
> To let go of fixation is the key point of liberation;
> When free from subtle attachment, you are a buddha.

※

Now, in accordance with the subject about which you inquire,

THE HEART OF THE MATTER

To describe the crucial points of and the
   dividing line between
Whether or not genuine realization has taken
   place,
Since I have previously often written about
The four yogas of Mahamudra and the four
   visions of Dzogchen, and so forth,
I shall not enumerate them again here.
Nevertheless, as the very heart of this matter,
I will explain the following in order to make
   the distinction
Between these two: experience and realization.

In the general vehicles including the Middle
   Way
The stages are described with many names,
   such as the thirty-seven aspects of
   enlightenment
Corresponding to the force of training in the
   samadhi of emptiness and compassion,

So I cannot explain them all here.
You can look for them in the major scriptures.

In any case, since all the categories of qualities belonging to gradual progress
On the paths and stages of the general vehicles
Are complete within this swift path,
And since you don't need to depend on such words if you accomplish it's nature,
I will set aside such elaborations.

In this system, during the four yogas and so forth,
To gain confidence in the indivisible unity
Of the essence of the training and your mind,
Is called the 'dawn of realization' and is itself enough.

Until that happens, as long as you maintain that the practice in which you train
Is separate from mind, the meditator,

Or that the sustainer of mindfulness is
    different from the object sustained,
You have still not glimpsed the heart of
    realization.

Therefore bliss, clarity or nonthought,
No matter what occurs — all these meditation-
    moods and experiences —
Are nothing but the outer 'peels' of the
    meditation training,
So they are never to be fondly clung to.

The uninterrupted experience of greater one-
    pointedness,
The simplicity of everything dawning as
    emptiness, and so forth
Are all nothing but meditation-moods and
    experiences — so give up conceit!

The meditator and the meditation object are
    the mind itself.

Distraction and mindfulness are both mind as well.

Good thoughts and bad thoughts are all the mind itself.

Recognizing the natural face is also this mind itself.

Once you resolve that everything is solely your own mind,

It is easy to realize the view of indivisible samsara and nirvana.

Once you resolve the root and basis of the view within yourself,

There is no meditation object apart from this single awareness.

Since it is never separate from you throughout the three times,

It is indeed not hard to have realization.

Nevertheless, the meditator who isn't resolved about mind,

Though meditating for a hundred aeons, will still cling to the meditation-moods.

Due to this clinging, which is the sole root cause of samsara,

There is no way to realize the fruition of Mahamudra or Dzogchen.

All classifications and dividing points are included within this.

☙❦❧

True realization is when you are free from the peels of the meditation-moods.

Though named 'realization,' it is uncorrupted awareness itself.

This uncorrupted awareness, your natural state,

Is itself the single aim of practice.

Because of different capacities, higher, medium and lesser
There can be rapid realization, gradual realization, and so forth.
But if you simply continue training until perfection,
You will be liberated into the primordial ground of the 'exhaustion of phenomena and concepts'.

Just like someone who has recovered from an epidemic,
You have no fear of again being deluded into samsara.
Having perfected the kayas and wisdoms, as well as the training,
An effortless compassion will spontaneously accomplish the welfare of beings.

Condensed to the essence, this ordinary mind,

Should be left as it naturally is and nothing else.

Striving for an eminent view and meditation, training in artifice,

Desiring experiences and realization, and to progress through the paths and stages of the yogas

While fearing going astray or taking sidetracks, and so forth,

Totally abandon all such pursuits.

☙❧

Lord Götsangpa said, "To condense everything into one point, I will simply practice this unimpaired present ordinary mind until reaching the state of buddhahood." Besides following this statement of his, don't harbor ambitions about anything else whatsoever.

The supreme being and lord of the Dharma (Chöje Rinpoche) said:

> Some accept that when the steadiness of the meditation state
> Has become continuous with
> The unbroken luminosity of the post-meditation,
> Is itself the realization of the buddha-mind.
>
> This is exactly what I too have understood:
> That the nakedness of ordinary mind is the dharmakaya
> In which both meditation and post-meditation, along with habitual tendencies,
> Are forever vanquished, like iron filed totally away.

He continued:

> While striving for qualities, you get stuck in the viscous disease of ambition.
> While trying to acquire a fruition, it is destroyed by the frost of expectations.
> While wishing for signs of progress, you get caught in the trap of Mara.

It is just as he has taught.

THE HEART OF THE MATTER

Though numerous types of conduct for enhancement are taught,
Including equal taste and yogic disciplines,
When you simply tame your own stream-of-being
You have no need for any other equal taste.

These days, all practitioners claim,
"I'm a meditator!, I'm a yogi!, I'm a mendicant!"
While chasing donations given out of faith.
They may wear the right costumes,
But when meeting the slightest disrespect, given measly offerings
Or hearing even the smallest criticism,
They forget their meditation and spiritual practice,
And, like a viper, fly into a rage.

How can there be any progress in their
    spiritual practice?
For such people, what is the use of equal taste?

Therefore it is not at all necessary
To live in scary solitudes
Or to engage in the yogic disciplines of
    pursuing confrontations;
Rather, it is most eminent, though very rare,
To exclusively live by the key point
Of a spiritual practice that transcends the eight
    worldly concerns.

Once a meditator from the Drigung school who claimed to have perfected the practice of illusory body was told by Kyobpa Rinpoche, "People say you have broken your vows; that is extremely offensive." When he got furious, Kyobpa Rinpoche said, "Since you claimed to have perfected the illusory body, I was testing you." The story goes that through this his pride was reduced.

Gyalsey Togmey Rinpoche also said:

> When my belly is full and the sun shines, I look like a practitioner.
> When confronting adversity I am an ordinary person.
> Since my mind has not mingled with the Dharma,
> Grant your blessings that my heart may be flexible.

As he said, this is obviously something to revere a hundred times at the crown of your head.

※

Furthermore, unless the Dharma tames your mind, there is no benefit in merely wearing the attire of a yogi or a monk. The *Udana Varga* mentions:

> The Blessed One addressed the monks, "How can the shaving of a monk's head

possibly be enlightenment? How can yellow robes possibly be enlightenment? How can rinsing oneself with water possibly be enlightenment? How can refraining from taking meals after noon possibly be enlightenment?"

His followers grew doubtful and uncertain and then said, "That being so, through what does one attain enlightenment?"

The Buddha replied, "Shave the hair of conceptual thinking with the razor of discriminating knowledge. Protect yourself from the aches of disturbing emotions with the robes of emptiness. Rinse away your ignorance with the water of wisdom. Dispel the hunger of desire with the food of meditation."

Here is how the awakened state is never attained simply through vast learning or extensive understanding unless one's mind is mingled with the

Dharma. To quote, the *Sutra of Nonorigination of Dharmas* says:

> Correct behavior and the rectification of
>   mistakes,
> Fondness of words and talk — none of these
>   indicate purity.
> Unless you fully comprehend the nature of
>   the truth,
> You don't awaken to enlightenment through
>   exactness in words.

The Buddha Avatamsaka Sutra mentions:

> The true teachings of the Buddha
> Are not accomplished through learning
>   alone.
> While forcibly carried away by a river
> Feeble people may still die of thirst.
> The teaching you fail to practice is similar to
>   this.

The same text continues:

> The steersman of a boat or ship
> On a river or on the ocean
> Though able to ferry others across,

May still die on the water himself.
The teaching you fail to practice is similar to this.

In this way it is has been taught in numerous other texts.

※

Most people, including myself, who nowadays claim to be practitioners, are nothing but what the conqueror Yang-gönpa describes in his *Advice*:

> All of us who follow the side of Dharma, unable to practice during even a single night's sleep, during the actions of even a single day or even during a short activity, occupy ourselves exclusively with achievements for this life. When we feel like practicing the sacred Dharma, we do it; when we don't feel like it, we suspend it. Sometimes, when it is convenient, we do it; when not, we suspend it.
>
> We wish to meditate without spending time learning how. We wish to have signs of

accomplishment without spending time in meditation training. With no time to practice the Dharma, we wish to immediately be a siddha or a *tokden*,[3] to have superknowledges and miraculous powers or to be something extraordinary.

When this doesn't happen, we interrupt our Dharma practice, discouraging ourselves by thinking, "Someone like me cannot possibly have success in practice." We all want to be enlightened without meditating or practicing, but it just won't happen!

He also said:

We need to take up a diligent course of action and practice throughout day and night. We may pretend to be someone who lives in a mountain hermitage and does retreat. We may feign being a good meditator, while chatting all day and sleeping all night. When we come out of retreat and go down from the mountain hermitage, we have neither progressed nor advanced in our spiritual practice. In mind and character we are still totally rigid and uptight. To be a

Dharma practitioner in appearance only won't help at all.

He said as well:

> You may have met with a master who is like the Buddha in person, received the nectar-like oral instructions and possess a meditation that is like Kailash, the king of snow mountains. Still, you won't be enlightened unless you also tame your mind. The meditator surely needs to have experiences and realization. Yet apart from meditating, no one will come along to give them to him.

He gave lots of similar advice all of which is only too true.

Once again, unless you can chiefly practice the very heart of the Dharma, it will be difficult to find something else that brings accomplishment. The *Sutra of the Good Aeon* states:

Besides abiding in the true practice,
You will not attain supreme enlightenment
   by any other means.

As just said, if you can focus on practicing the profound key points of oral instruction, you effectively use the essence of all the teachings in full. The *Sutra of the King of Samadhi* describes this:

Whichever sutra I have taught
In all the world systems,
The words have but a single meaning.
You cannot practice all of them,
But by practicing just a single sentence,
You will be practicing them all.

It is exactly as the Buddha just said. This being so, it is not necessary to immediately have visible signs of special traits or good qualities, but rather, to accomplish all true needs and thereby attain what is of lasting value. The Precious Master of Uddiyana said:

Empty awareness can in no way be harmed by external things nor can any adversity obstruct it. By resolving the nature of samsara, you won't find any basis for taking rebirth among the six classes of beings. By capturing the fabric of thought within the nature of instantaneous awareness, the evil zombie of disturbing emotions cannot possibly rise up again within unconditioned empty cognizance. By bringing the roots of karmic ripening to exhaustion, misdeeds are swept away. By being free from re-occurrence of body and speech, the inroads to the lower realms are blocked. By recognizing all that appears and exists to be mind, the hells are utterly nonexistent. When meeting with such oral instructions, the person who practices unwaveringly and one-pointedly doesn't need to fear death, since within this life he has already accomplished the task of lasting value.

For this to happen you need to exert yourself.

༄༅༔

Therefore, all of you who intend to make use of these freedoms and riches,

Follow a sublime spiritual teacher and resolve uncertainty about the instructions.

Reflect sincerely upon your mortality and cast away attachment to this world.

Equalize the eight worldly concerns and mingle your minds with the Dharma.

As the essence of view and meditation, sustain naked awareness.

As the essence of daily activities, follow the example of the masters of the Practice Lineage.

As the essence of precepts and samayas, don't belittle the law of cause and effect.

As the essence of activity, subdue the evil spirit of selfishness.

Don't stray into nihilistic dissipation; bring the teachings into actual practice.

Don't pursue details with attachment; realize everything to be like a magical illusion.

Don't bind yourself in the chains of duality; be carefree and unfettered.

It is extremely important to understand the key points of the Dharma.

Alas! In this dark age when all afflictions coincide,

And the chariot of the Buddha's teachings sinks into the muddy swamp,

No matter how much you intend to work for the benefit of the teachings,

It is hopeless to expect it to truly help the Buddhadharma.

The sectarianism of upholding your personal philosophical view,

The business of maintaining a monastery and keeping followers,

The devices for acquiring the necessities of funds and food,

Cause nothing but personal regret and others' scorn.

Meaningless words and worldly learning,
Volumes of information, and the pretentious aims of fame and material gain,
Maintaining the artificial guise of a master which ruins both self and others,
I make the wish to never again pursue any of these.

In forests and unpeopled valleys, as praised by the Buddha,
With the renunciation of knowing that nothing is needed,
May I and all others without exception exert ourselves
In facing the original buddha of our own minds.

By the power of the virtue of writing down, with pure motivation,

THE HEART OF THE MATTER

The vital points for embarking on the essential view and meditation of all the teachings
Supported by the statements spoken by the victorious ones,
May the ocean of samsara quickly dry up and may all beings attain enlightenment!

☙❧

Though I have written this in response to a request from the monk Mönlam who expressed the need for such notes on the key points for practicing the view and meditation of the profound path of Mahamudra, Dzogchen, and Madhyamika, I personally possess neither definitive experience nor realization, so this will hardly be in accordance with their exact meaning. All I have expressed here may be nothing more than nonsense, like the babbling of someone drunk on wine. Nevertheless, I wrote this with the single pure intention of benefiting others, free from any extraneous defilements.

THE HEART OF THE MATTER

So as to be easily understood by everyone, both high and low, and avoiding the flowery words of poetics, I have emphasized straightforward meaning in ordinary language. In this cliff-overhang hermitage of Götsangpa's cave, I, Natsok Rangdröl, wrote this at the auspicious event of the first day of the waxing part of the second month. Through the outcome of this virtue may all beings reach perfection in their endeavors on a profound path such as this. May it be virtuous!

☸

༄༅། །འཆི་མེད་རིག་འཛིན་ཆེན་པོ་སྐུ་མྱ་ངན་ཆོས་ཀྱི་དབྱིངས་སུ་
གཤེགས་ཁར་གནང་བའི་ཞལ་གདམས་བཞུགས་སོ། །

The Final Words

ORAL INSTRUCTION GIVEN BY THE GREAT
VIDYADHARA OF IMMORTALITY WHEN ABOUT TO
DEPART INTO DHARMADHATU

At all times and in all situations, I bow to and take refuge in the sublime qualified master endowed with boundless compassion who is like a wish-fulfilling jewel! Please bestow your blessings upon me!

To attain the state of unexcelled enlightenment, upon entering the gate of the precious Buddhadharma, you must give up concerns for this life!

Your parents, family, friends and other people lead your mind towards the fleeting goals of this life's activities, involving you in countless temporary and ultimate schemes, and offering all kinds of seemingly affectionate advice. Fooling yourself with all this will only result in various hindrances for Dharma practice, so it is essential not to listen to their words!

Besides a qualified master you won't find anyone who can give genuine spiritual advice. If you want to truly practice the Dharma you must quickly make preparations for death. Besides that, someone who entertains many temporary and ultimate plans will not be able to be a Dharma practitioner. People nowadays may outwardly pretend to try to please everyone but that only proves they are possessed inwardly by Mara.

Place your trust in the Dharma and your master! Take mountain retreats and unpeopled valleys as your dwelling place! Give up clinging to the short-lived pleasures of food, clothes and the like! Cut your ties to close family members! Cast away all hypocritical flattery and manipulation! Focus one-pointedly on whatever your master says! By doing so your Dharma practice will be pure.

In general, people nowadays fall under Mara's reign. In particular, fickle and indolent women don't follow the advice of their teachers and instead take guidance from their family. By doing so they postpone doing what they definitely should be doing now: studying and training in Dharma practice. They seem to be primarily caught up in pointless worldly activities, kow-towing to family and friends, and the like. Therefore take hold of the "rope to your nose" and don't listen to others!

Sincerely take to heart the fact that the time of death lies uncertain. Then, knowing that there is no time to waste, diligently apply yourself to spiritual practice!

Your parent's kindness can only be repaid through Dharma practice; there is no benefit in repaying them with mundane attainments. Your teacher's kindness can only be repaid by practicing meditation, nothing else will do.

You can only benefit sentient beings through the bodhichitta resolve and by making aspirations; comparatively, any other immediate action is of little benefit. As for your vows and samayas, unless you take your own conscience as witness, you will only become a hypocrite even though you may maintain a superficially virtuous morality and exterior.

Remain in secluded valleys and mountain retreats, because any spiritual practice done among the masses will only get you caught up in one situation after another. If you fail to take control of your own mind, even though you may make many promises and take many vows, they will result in hardly any benefit at all.

Unless you realize the key point of natural awareness — that knowing one thing liberates all — you won't find any certainty in pursuing endless seemingly 'important' information.

To summarize all vital points: with the thought "I will surely die!", hasten your plans to practice the Dharma! Since a master is your only hope, supplicate him from your heart! Since all pleasure and pain, whatever befalls you, is a repayment from the past, don't entertain many plans! Treat good, evil and impartial people as being above you and always take the lowest seat!

Train in impartial pure perception and do not belittle others! Acknowledge your own faults, and don't meditate on others' shortcomings! Since the vital point of all the teachings lies in your own mind, always scrutinize it's nature!

Cast away the fixation of rigidly meditating upon a reference point and instead release your awareness into carefree openness! Decide that whatever you experience is the playful expression of awareness; don't try to improve good or correct evil!

All experience is your own mind, and this mind, free from arising and ceasing, is the identity of the trikaya guru. This guru is indivisible from your natural awareness. Its cognizant radiance encompasses all that appears and exists.

Since all of appearance and existence is the magical display of this single expanse of awareness, the 'ultimate view' is to see your mind in utterly naked naturalness. 'Meditation training' is to remain in this continuously. 'Ensuing cognition' is when a thought is projected. 'Post-meditation' is to recognize that projection. 'Conduct' is to mingle walking, sitting, and all other activities with the state of awareness.

The indivisibility of meditation and post-meditation is to be continuously free from even a second of distraction or confusion, uninterrupted by gaps of stillness or thought occurrence. When perfected it is the indivisibility of appearance and mind, of self and others, of pleasure and pain, enmity and friendship, and of love and hate. In short, 'fruition' is to have perpetually exhausted all kinds of duality-fixating concepts.

When that has happened, samsara and nirvana are purified into the space [of dharmadhatu] and you have realized the spontaneously present three kayas. This is called 'attaining buddhahood,' the 'exhaustion of phenomena and concepts' or 'becoming a siddha'. This is the time of gaining mastery over birth and death and the physical elements, and when effortless compassion and activity spontaneously occur throughout the entire universe.

In brief, the basic cause of everything is nothing but your present natural awareness. Therefore, the sublime key point is to continuously maintain your natural awareness throughout both day and night without any separation.

As for all the thoughts that do occur as the expression of this natural awareness, be they gross or subtle, don't analyze them and don't follow them either. Don't try to bring them back into your meditation or obstruct them. If you succeed in simply recognizing the sudden occurrence of a thought, then let be in just that.

When it happens that you do get involved in thoughts that recollect the past or entertain the future, then let be directly in awareness. If a thought pattern continues, there is no need for a separate antidote since whatever takes place is liberated by itself. What occurs spontaneously is the radiance of your own mind. To see it with vivid clarity is the essential instruction!

It is your mind's natural disposition to spontaneously reflect. Consequently, spend your life within this state of carefree and pervasive openness, of undistracted nonmeditation, of knowing one thing that liberates all — in which all that appears and exists is dharmakaya, samsara and nirvana are indivisible, and arising and liberation are simultaneous. If you spend your entire life in spiritual activities within this kind of state, in which the thinker and the object of thought are an undivided unity, there is not a single doubt that you will capture the 'stronghold of non-regression' in this very life.

> Wherever the person stays who has
>   abandoned all activities,
> That very place is the buddhafield.
> If you can supplicate without duplicity,
> All that appears and exists is then the guru's
>   mandala.
>
> As soon as you cut the root of the demon
>   Ego-clinging,
> You are permanently free from obstacles,
>   misfortune and Mara.
> The moment you understand that the guru is
>   indivisible from your own mind,
> The falsehood of superficial meeting and
>   separation spontaneously collapses.
>
> Once you resolve that samsara and nirvana
>   are the display of awareness,
> Who is there to experience the pain of any
>   lower realm?
> When realizing that your natural awareness is
>   the primordially free dharmakaya,

What is the point of entertaining hopes and
    fears about the paths and bhumis?

In the meeting of the already acquainted
    mother and child luminosities,
What is the use of fearing the collapse of the
    illusory body?
When dying, die within the primordially pure
    space of luminosity!
While alive, there is nothing more important
    than training in meditation with
    unflagging constancy!

You may compare all the sutras, tantras and
    oral instructions,
But the essence of realization is nothing
    other than this!
The ultimate and essential heart advice is
    precisely this!
And my last words at death are also none
    other than this!

All worthy ones who are devoted to me,
Don't pay lip-service to this, but assimilate
    its meaning!

The experience of original wakefulness will
    then dawn from within your hearts,
And you will arrive at buddhahood in a single
    instant!

By whatever merit which might arise from
    this advice,
May all my old mothers, sentient beings
    filling the whole of space, be liberated!
Mangalam.

Translator's Afterword

Through the kind guidance of Kyabje Tulku Urgyen Rinpoche and his eminent son, Chökyi Nyima Rinpoche, this feeble attempt of a translation was made at Pal Rangjung Yeshe kyi Gomdé in Denmark and completed at Nagi Gompa in Nepal by Erik Pema Kunsang. It was finalized with the help of Khenpo Chadrel and Lama Putsi Pema Tashi. The text was compared with the Tibetan by Marcia Binder Schmidt, and edited by Michael Tweed. Thanks to S. Lhamo for proof-reading.

By the power of the aspirations of Tsele Natsok Rangdröl, may this book be a direct cause of furthering the practice of the Buddha's teachings and of bringing benefit to countless beings.

These texts were translated for use at the yearly seminar conducted by Rangjung Yeshe Institute at Pal Ka-Nying Shedrub Ling Monastery, Boudhanath, Kathmandu, Nepal.

Tsele Natsok Rangdröl is also the author of *Mirror of Mindfulness*, *Lamp of Mahamudra*, *Empowerment*, and *Circle of the Sun*.

Masters and Texts Quoted

Asanga (thogs med). Great Indian scholar; chiefly associated with the Mind Only School.

Buddha Avatamsaka Sutra (sangs rgyas phal po che). English title: *The Flower Adornment Sutra*, Shambhala Publ.

Cutting (gcod). One of the eight Practice Lineages of Tibet; connected to Machik Labdrön.

Dzogchen Hearing Lineage of Aro (rdzogs pa chen po a ro'i snyan brgyud). Focusing on the Mind Section of the Great Perfection; lineage transmitted through Aro Yeshe Jungney.

Gampopa (mnyam med sgam po pa). Early Kagyü master, disciple of Milarepa and teacher of the first Karmapa and Phagmo Drubpa. Author of

Golden Garland of Rulu (ru lu gser phreng).

Götsangpa, the conqueror (rgyal ba rgod tshang pa). 1189-1258. Early Drukpa Kagyü master.

Gyalsey Togmey Rinpoche (rgyal sras rin po che thogs med) 1295-1369. A great Kadampa master and author of the famous *37 Practices of a Bodhisattva*. Also known as Ngülchu Togmey Zangpo (dngul chu thogs med bzang po).

THE HEART OF THE MATTER

Gyalwa Drigungpa (rgyal ba bri gung pa).

Hashang (hva shang). Chinese Mahayana teacher.

Khachö Lutreng (mkha' spyod klu 'phreng).

Kyobpa Rinpoche (skyobs pa rin pa che). 1143-1217. Early master in the Drigung Kagyü lineage.; disciple of Phagmo Drubpa.

Lalita Vistara (rgya cher rol pa, *Sutra of the Vast Display*). A biography of Buddha Shakyamuni. English title: *The Voice of the Buddha*, Dharma Publishing.

Lingje Repa (gling rje ras pa). 1128-88. Early Drukpa Kagyü master.

Luhipa, the siddha (grub thob lu hi pa). Indian mahasiddha.

Maitreya (byams pa). The bodhisattva disciple of Buddha Shakyamuni, teacher of Asanga and the next buddha to appear in this aeon.

Maitripa (mai tri pa). An Indian siddha in the Mahamudra lineage who was the guru of Naropa.

Manjushri ('jam dpal dbyangs). The bodhisattva disciple of Buddha Shakyamuni; personifying transcendent knowledge and the view of the Middle Way.

Marpa, lord (rje mar pa). 1012-1097. Founder of the Kagyü tradition in Tibet. Disciple of Naropa and teacher of Milarepa.

Milarepa (mi la ras pa). 1040-1123. The great Tibetan yogi; disciple of Marpa and teacher of Gampopa; known for his *Hundred Thousand Songs* and biography.

Nagarjuna (klu grub). Great Indian scholar; chiefly associated with the Middle Way School.

Naropa, the glorious (dpal na ro pa). Indian pandita, siddha and teacher of Marpa.

Noble Eight Thousand Verses ('phags pa brgyad stong pa). The middle length Prajnaparamita sutra.

Nyang Ben Tingdzin Zangpo (nyang ban ting 'dzin bzang po). Tibetan master; disciple of Vimalamitra and Padmasambhava.

Orgyenpa, the siddha (grub thob o rgyan pa). 1230-1309. A disciple of Gyalwa Götsangpa and the second Karmapa, Karma Pakshi.

Pacifying (zhi byed). One of the eight Practice Lineages in Tibet; connected to the Indian mahasiddha Padampa Sangye.

Phagmo Drubpa, the sugata (bde gshegs phag mo grub pa). 1110-70. Disciple of Gampopa.

Precious Master of Uddiyana (o rgyan rin po che). Padmasambhava; the great Lotus-Born guru; founder of Buddhism in Tibet.

Sakyapa, Lord (rje sa skya pa). 1182-1251. Also known as Sakya Pandita Kunga Gyaltsen; early master of the Sakya lineage.

Samantabhadra (kun tu bzang po). The dharmakaya buddha in the Dzogchen lineage.

Saraha (bram ze chen po sa ra ha). Indian mahasiddha in the Mahamudra lineage; famous for his songs.

Shang Rinpoche ('gro mgon zhang rin po che / zhang g.yu brag mgon po). 1123-1193. Founder of Tsalpa Kagyü.

Shavaripa (dpal sha wa ra). Indian master. Student of Nagarjuna and teacher of Maitripa.

Subhuti (rab 'byor). Among the ten chief shravaka attendants of Buddha Shakyamuni, the one famed for eminence in teaching emptiness.

Sutra of Nonorigination of Dharmas (chos 'byung ba med pa'i mdo).

Sutra of the Good Aeon (mdo sde bskal bzang). Dharma Publishing.

Sutra of the King of Samadhi (ting 'dzin rgyal po'i mdo). See also *King of Samadhi*, Thrangu Rinpoche, Rangjung Yeshe Publ.

Sutra on Pure Intention (bsam pa dag pa'i mdo).

Tilopa (til li pa). Indian mahasiddha; teacher of Naropa.

Udana Varga (ched du brjod pa'i tshom). A Mahayana version of the Pali *Dammapada*.

Vimalamitra (dri med gshes gnyen). Indian pandita and mahasiddha; one of three masters to bring Dzogchen teachings to Tibet.

Yang-gönpa, the conqueror (rgyal ba yang dgon pa). 1213-1287. Drukpa Kagyü master; disciple of Götsangpa.

Notes

[1]. The name of the one who requested this teaching is Aspiration, Mönlam.
[2]. Being too involved in giving clear predictions to people is like being overtaken by the power of evil spirits. The is nothing especially amazing about mundane powers.
[3]. Tokden means 'realized one'. Often this title is used for someone who has gained accomplishment in the Six Yogas of Naropa.